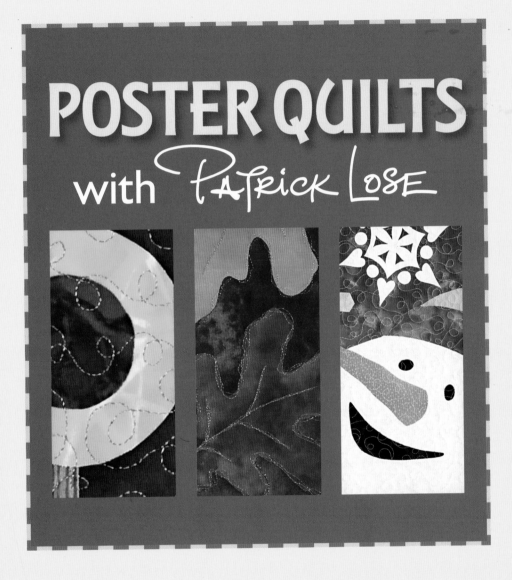

POSTER QUILTS
with Patrick Lose

C&T PUBLISHING

Library of Congress Cataloging-in-Publication Data
Lose, Patrick.
  Poster quilts with Patrick Lose : 10 festive, fusible quilts for year-round fun / Patrick Lose.
     p. cm.
  Summary: "Quilted wallhangings and banners in the fun and distinctive Patrick Lose style. Holiday and seasonal themes feature ten fusible appliqué projects that are fast and easy to make"--Provided by publisher.
  ISBN 978-1-57120-653-4 (paper trade : alk. paper)
  1. Appliqué--Patterns. 2. Quilting--Patterns. 3. Wall hangings 4. Banners. I. Title.
  TT779.L675 2009
  746.44'5041--dc22
                              2008040761
Printed in China

10 9 8 7 6 5 4 3 2 1

ACKNOWLEDGMENTS

For their assistance in making the projects in this book, I'd like to thank the following people:

Gary Rushton, Katie Fjell, Lauryn "Lulu" Fjell, Sharron Meyer, Nora Hart, Denissa Schulman, Beverly Bruder, Candy Norris, and Susanne Triplett.

I'd also like to say thanks to Darlene Ros, the owner of Quiltz in Phoenix, Arizona, for providing the classroom at her shop for our "Project Party" and to Karen Petry and Tori Ros for organizing it.

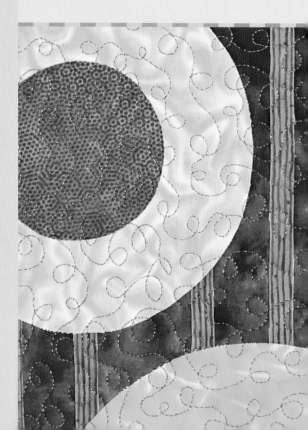

CONTENTS

INTRODUCTION

We all wish there was more time to do the things we enjoy doing, but quilting often takes a backseat to the more pressing day-to-day activities. How often have you wished you had the time to make a door banner or wallhanging to display or give as a gift to celebrate an occasion? There's no reason to spend hours and hours making something that's used for short periods of time during the year. If you want to spend all that time quilting, at least have several pieces to show for it instead of one!

That's why I wanted to create this book of projects: to offer some designs for seasonal pieces that would be fast and easy to make. An experienced quilter could make any of these appliqué projects in a day with fusible adhesive and free-motion quilting. I would have made all of them using a raw-edge technique, but satin-stitch appliqué was needed for a couple of projects because they needed more stitching detail to complete the design. It's up to you which method of appliqué you want to use, based on the time you have available to spend on the project. If you use a good fusible adhesive and fairly dense quilting over the design, I can assure you that your appliqués will last for years to come.

I hope you enjoy making these projects as much as my friends and I did. And I wish you many happy seasons of displaying them.

Patrick

GENERAL INSTRUCTIONS

As tempting as it may be to jump right into your project, read the instructions thoroughly before you begin working. All the projects in *Poster Quilts* are pieced using a ¼″-wide seam allowance, with the fabrics placed right sides together.

TOOLS

Make sure you have all the necessary tools at hand before you start cutting and stitching up a storm. It's easy to let your excitement for the project get the best of you, but then you'll be off to the quilt shop to buy more fabric or to hunt for a seam ripper. Following is a list of helpful tools that will make your stitching easier.

- Rotary cutter and cutting mat
- Transparent acrylic gridded ruler
- Sewing machine in good working order capable of doing a narrow zigzag or satin stitch
- Paper scissors
- Fabric scissors
- Sewing machine needles, size 80/12 universal Titanium needles are great but not necessary.
- Various threads for appliqué and quilting
- Iron and ironing board
- Darning foot for free-motion quilting
- Safety pins
- Lite Steam-A-Seam 2 fusible adhesive
- Lightweight tear-away stabilizer for satin-stitch appliqué

FABRICS

I don't prewash my fabrics for quilting. This is my personal preference, and I have never had a problem with colors bleeding. If I do wash the finished piece, the minimal shrinkage creates a slightly puckered quilt with a softer look and feel. Some people always prewash, and that is perfectly fine. Just be sure that if you prewash, you use warm water to allow the fabric to shrink as much as it is going to. Tumble dry the fabric, and remove it from the dryer when it is still slightly damp. Always iron the fabric before measuring and cutting. Do not use starch on fabrics that will be used for appliqué pieces. It could make the fabric difficult to fuse.

It is extremely important to measure and cut your fabrics accurately and to stitch using an exact ¼˝ seam allowance. I am certain you'll be proud of your finished piece if you follow these simple rules.

APPLIQUÉ

The appliqué projects in this book use a fused method. I've used raw-edge appliqué for most of the projects, but feel free to appliqué in your favorite method. Should you wish to do hand appliqué (knock yourself out), you'll need to trace the printed templates in mirror image and add seam allowances to them. Then you can lay them onto the right side of the fabric for cutting. You can also appliqué by outlining the pieces using a machine satin or zigzag stitch, such as I did in *Proud To Be Irish*, page 17, and *Halloween Hag*, page 33.

FUSIBLE APPLIQUÉ PREPARATIONS

Templates are printed actual size and are reversed for tracing onto fusible adhesive. Be sure to use a lightweight, paper-backed fusible adhesive that is suitable for sewing. I choose Lite Steam-A-Seam 2, because I know it stays fused over time in raw edge-appliqué. If necessary when tracing, join the pieces as indicated on the template.

1. Lay the fusible adhesive, paper side up, over each template piece, and trace the shape onto the paper side. It helps to write the name, piece number, and fabric color on each piece as you trace it.

> Note: In places where the pieces butt one another, overlapping them helps to keep them from gapping. Either you can cut the pieces exactly and then overlap by a hair, or (particularly if you are new to satin stitching) you can add approximately ¹⁄₁₆˝ to the underneath piece. Please note that the latter method will add some bulk to your project.

2. Use paper-cutting scissors to roughly cut all the pieces approximately ¼˝ outside the traced lines.

3. Following the manufacturer's instructions for the fusible adhesive, fuse the traced pattern piece(s) onto the wrong side of the fabric you've chosen for it.

4. Cut out the pieces neatly along the traced lines.

5. Transfer any placement and stitching lines to the right side of the fabric using a lightbox and a pencil.

6. Arrange all of the appliqués as pictured, and when you're satisfied with the arrangement, fuse them to the background.

LAYERING AND QUILTING

I like to use a single layer of thin cotton batting such as Warm & Natural. Cut your backing fabric and batting to measure an inch or two larger than your quilt top on all sides. Sandwich the batting between the quilt top and the backing, wrong sides together, and baste through all the layers, smoothing the quilt top outward from the center. You can also use safety pins spaced 4˝ to 6˝ apart.

All the quilting in this book was done by machine. I use a walking foot for straight-line quilting. For free-motion or stipple quilting, I use a darning foot and lower the feed dogs on my machine. Quilt as desired, or refer to the photos and quilting suggestions that are included with each project. A Clover Chaco Liner is great for marking quilting lines if you are not comfortable eyeballing them, and the chalk lines can be easily brushed away.

BINDING

The instructions for each project give you the amount of binding necessary to finish your quilt project.

1. Cut 2½˝-wide strips selvage to selvage using a rotary cutter, a mat, and a transparent acrylic gridded ruler.

2. Use diagonal seams to join the binding strips. Trim the seam allowances, and press the seams open.

Stitch

3. Fold the completed binding strip in half lengthwise with the wrong sides together. Press.

4. Place the folded binding strip on the right edge of the quilt top, beginning in the center of the edge and aligning the raw edges of the quilt and the binding. Fold over the beginning of the binding strip about ½˝. Stitch through all the layers using a ¼˝ seam allowance. Stop stitching ¼˝ from the corner. Backstitch at least 2 stitches, remove the quilt from the machine, and clip the threads.

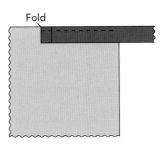

Fold

5. Fold up the binding, and crease the fold with your fingers.

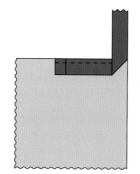

6. Holding the creased fold in place, fold the binding down and align the raw edges with the next side of the quilt. Start stitching again at the corner, through all the layers. Stitch around the entire quilt, treating each corner as you did the first.

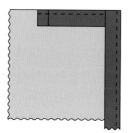

7. When you return to where you started, stitch the binding beyond the fold you made in the strip at the beginning. Backstitch at least 2 stitches, and clip the threads. Cut off the excess batting and backing fabric so that all the layers are even.

8. Turn the binding over the quilt edge, aligning the fold of the binding with the machine stitching you just finished. You can pin the binding in place, but I like to use those funny little hair clips that bend and then snap closed; they work great and don't prick your fingers or get stuck in the carpet. You can find them at most variety stores and drugstores, and fabric stores often carry them in the quilting notions section.

Hand sew the binding onto the backing, making sure you cover the machine stitching. Miter the corners on the back side of the quilt also, folding the miter in the opposite direction from the front fold.

If you choose to stitch the binding on the back by machine, lap the fold over the machine-stitching line used to attach the binding to the front. I use the same clips to hold the binding in place, miter my corners on the back, and stitch them into place by hand before going to the machine. Then stitch in the ditch from the front, catching the overlapped binding fold on the back. If I miss a spot or two, I just finish it by hand. After all, these quilts won't be entering any technique competitions!

Be sure to display your work of art in a conspicuous place where it is most likely to prompt compliments, but keep in mind that direct sunlight will fade fabric more quickly than you might think. Remember that because these projects are seasonal, you probably won't display them year-round. If you store them in cotton casings, not plastic, they should last to grace your home for many happy seasons.

ADDING A HANGING SLEEVE (OPTIONAL)

The yardage needed for the sleeve and the ribbon/cording will vary depending on the desired finished look you wish to achieve and the size of the project. These yardages are not included in the project material lists.

1. To hang the banner, you'll need to make a sleeve for the back to put a ½˝ dowel in. Cut a backing fabric piece to measure 3½˝ wide × the quilt width measurement.

2. Make a roll hem for each short side by folding under ¼˝ to the wrong side. Press. Fold under another ¼˝ and press. Stitch close to the folded edges.

3. Fold the piece lengthwise, right sides together, and stitch using a ¼˝-wide seam allowance. Turn it right side out and press. Slipstitch the long sides of this rectangle to the back of the banner, just under the binding. Insert the dowel to stabilize the top edge.

4. Sew a length of ribbon or decorative cord to the backside of the top corners of the quilt for hanging. Yardage will vary depending on the finished look you wish to achieve.

20″ × 24″ • Quilt top made by Denissa Schulman and Patrick Lose • Quilted by Patrick Lose

Colorful confetti and falling stars from your scrap stash
make for a festive welcome to the new year.

FABRIC AND SUPPLIES

Bright pink: 1 yard for binding strips, backing, large star, and confetti

Black: ½ yard for background and corner block

Blue: ¼ yard or fat quarter for vertical and horizontal border block

Gray: 10″ × 13″ rectangle for upper hourglass

Yellow: 9″ × 11″ rectangle for letters, medium star, and confetti

Brown: 8″ × 17″ rectangle for hourglass holder

Light gray: 6″ × 10″ rectangle for lower hourglass/sand

Green: 6″ × 6″ square for medium star and confetti

Lavender: 6″ × 6″ square for medium star and confetti

Orange: 4″ × 4″ square for small star and confetti

Batting: 23″ × 27″

Fusible adhesive (18″ wide): 1 yard

CUTTING FABRICS

From Bright Pink:

Cut 3 strips 2½″ × width of fabric for the binding.

Cut 1 rectangle 23″ × 27″ for the backing.

Cut 1 square 6″ × 6″ for the large star and confetti.

From Black:

Cut 1 rectangle 16½″ × 20½″ for the background.

Cut 1 square 4½″ × 4½″ for the corner block.

From Blue:

Cut 1 rectangle 4½″ × 20½″ for the vertical border block.

Cut 1 rectangle 4½″ × 16½″ for the horizontal border block.

CREATING THE APPLIQUÉS

All the appliqué template pieces are in the pullout section. They are printed actual size and are reversed for tracing onto fusible adhesive. Refer to Fusible Appliqué Preparations, pages 6–7, for instructions.

1. Lay the fusible adhesive, paper side up, over each appliqué template, and trace the shape onto the paper. Leave approximately ¼˝ of cutting space around each traced piece. Trace as many as indicated by the number on each template. Feel free to trace and make as many confetti pieces as you like.

 You can also iron fusible adhesive to the wrong sides of some of the scrap fabrics in your stash and cut them as desired to make your confetti.

2. Use paper-cutting scissors to roughly cut out all of the pieces outside the traced lines.

3. Following the manufacturer's instructions for fusing, fuse the traced template pieces, paper side up, onto the wrong side of the fabrics you've chosen for your appliqués. Don't fuse until all the pieces are arranged to fit on the fabrics.

4. Neatly cut out all of the appliqués from the fused fabrics.

PIECING THE BANNER

1. Stitch one of the long sides of the vertical border block to one of the long sides of the background block, right sides together, using a ¼˝-wide seam. Press the seam allowance toward the border.

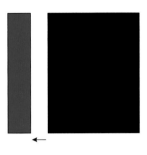

2. Stitch one side of the corner block to one of the short sides of the horizontal border block, right sides together, using a ¼˝-wide seam. Press the seam allowance toward the border.

3. Stitch the 2 pieces together to complete the top. Press the seam allowance toward the bottom border.

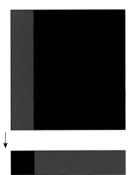

POSITIONING AND FUSING THE APPLIQUÉS

1. Remove the paper backing from the appliqués.

2. Referring to the project photo, page 9, arrange all of the appliqués on the quilt top. When centering the letters and the corner block's star, remember that there is a ¼˝-wide seam allowance on all sides for the binding.

3. When you're satisfied with the arrangement of the appliqués, fuse them into place. Always follow the fusible adhesive manufacturer's instructions.

QUILTING AND FINISHING

1. Sandwich the batting between the quilt top and backing, and quilt as desired. If necessary, refer to Layering and Quilting, page 7. I used black thread and free-motion quilting in a fairly dense loopy path over the entire quilt.

2. Finish the banner with the bright pink binding strips by following the instructions in Binding, pages 7–8.

POP HEARTS

22″ × 22″ • Quilt top made by Gary Rushton and Patrick Lose • Quilted by Patrick Lose

I wanted to create a heart-themed quilt with a pop art feel
for Valentine's Day. You might even consider matting and
framing the top rather than quilting it.

FABRIC AND SUPPLIES

Black: 1 yard (44″–45″ wide fabric) for the backing, borders, heart outlines, and binding

Nine colors of your choice: One 8″ × 12″ rectangle of each color for the background and heart (I used pink, grape, yellow, blue, red, light blue, orange, violet, and lime.)

Batting: 25″ × 25″

Fusible adhesive (18″ wide): 1 yard

CUTTING FABRICS

From Black:

Use a rotary cutter and straightedge to remove the selvage from one side of the fabric. Parallel to this edge, cut 7 strips 2½″ × width of fabric. Three of these strips will be used for the binding, and 4 will be used for the borders.

Cut 1 square 25″ × 25″ for the backing. This will leave a rectangle, when trimmed, from which you'll fuse and cut the 9 heart outline templates.

Selvage

Trimmed selvage edge

From the Nine Colors:

From each of the 9 remaining colors, cut a square 6½″ × 6½″, leaving enough fabric to also cut a heart template.

PIECING THE QUILT TOP

1. Join the 9 blocks that make the background by stitching them together in rows first, then stitching the rows together. Stitch the fabric right sides together, using a ¼˝-wide seam allowance. Press.

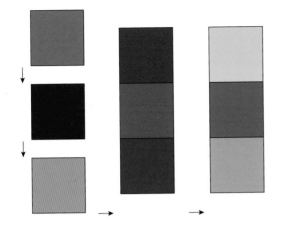

2. Piece the borders onto the Nine-Patch background. With right sides together, stitch one of the black 2½˝ -wide strips to the right side of the background. Press toward the border. Trim the excess using a rotary cutter and straightedge aligned with the background.

3. Stitch another border strip to the left side of the background in the same manner, press, and trim.

4. Repeat Steps 2 and 3 to add the top and bottom borders, trimming them to align with the raw edges of the right and left borders. Press.

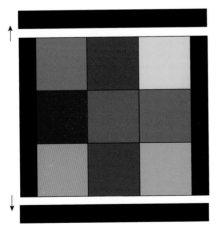

CREATING THE APPLIQUÉS

All of the appliqué templates are in the pullout section. They are printed actual size and are reversed for tracing onto fusible adhesive. Refer to Fusible Appliqué Preparations, pages 6–7, for instructions.

1. Lay the fusible adhesive, paper side up, over the heart and heart outline appliqué templates, and trace the shapes onto the paper side 9 times. Leave approximately ¼˝ of space around each piece for cutting.

2. Use paper-cutting scissors to roughly cut out all of the pieces outside the traced lines.

3. Following the manufacturer's instructions for fusing, fuse the traced heart outline template pieces, paper side up, onto the wrong side of the remaining black fabric. Don't fuse them until all of the pieces are arranged to fit on the fabric.

4. In the same way, fuse a heart to the wrong sides of what remains of each of the 9 fabrics used for your background blocks.

5. Neatly cut out all of the appliqués from the fused fabrics.

POSITIONING AND FUSING THE APPLIQUÉS

1. Remove the paper backing from the appliqués.

2. Referring to the project photo, page 13, center a heart in each of the 9 blocks. Be sure to place the fusible side of the fabric against the block. Finger-press them into place.

3. Place one of the heart outline appliqués onto each of the hearts, centering them so that the raw edges of the hearts are not visible.

4. When you're satisfied with the arrangement of the appliqués, fuse them into place. Always follow the fusible adhesive manufacturer's instructions.

QUILTING AND FINISHING

1. Sandwich the batting between the quilt top and backing, and quilt as desired. If necessary, refer to Layering and Quilting, page 7. I used black thread and what I call "scribble" stitching to free-motion quilt over each of the hearts. I also made several passes in a wavy grid formation over the seams of the 9 blocks and used the same wavy lines to quilt the borders.

2. Bind the banner with the remaining black strips by following the instructions in Binding, pages 7-8.

PROUD TO BE IRISH

18˝ × 28˝ • Quilt top made by Candy Norris and Patrick Lose • Quilted by Patrick Lose

Here's a banner to show off your Irish pride when
St. Patrick's Day rolls around again. After all, that's
the one day when everyone's Irish!

FABRIC AND SUPPLIES

Green: 1 yard for letters, rainbow strip, backing, and binding

Blue: ⅓ yard for Irish background

Five colors for rainbow: One ⅛ yard each of red, orange, yellow, turquoise, and purple

Gold: 6″ × 10″ rectangle for coins

Black: 11″ × 14″ rectangle for pot

Gray: 3″ × 5″ rectangle for pot highlight

Batting: 21″ × 31″

Fusible adhesive (18″ wide): ¾ yard

CUTTING FABRICS

From Green:

Cut 3 strips 2½″ × width of fabric for the binding.

Cut 1 strip 2″ × 28″ for the rainbow.

From Blue:

Cut 1 rectangle 9″ × 28″ for the background.

From the Rainbow Colors:

From each of the 5 remaining colors, cut a 2″ × 28″ strip for the rainbow.

PIECING THE QUILT TOP

In all of the steps below, all stitching is done with the right sides of the fabrics together and using a ¼″-wide seam allowance.

1. Stitch one of the long sides of the red rainbow strip to one of the long sides of the orange strip. Press toward the red strip.

2. Stitch the remaining long side of the orange strip to one of the long sides of the yellow strip. Press. Continue piecing the rainbow together in this manner. Press all of the seams toward the red strip.

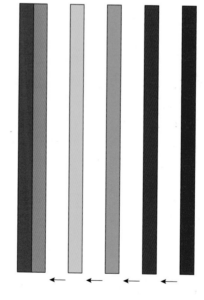

3. Stitch the long red side of this rainbow block to one of the long sides of the blue piece. Press the seam toward the blue.

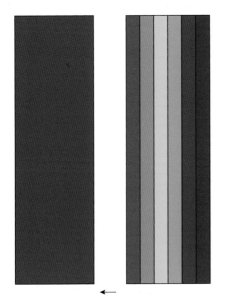

CREATING THE APPLIQUÉS

All appliqué templates are in the pullout section. They are printed actual size and are reversed for tracing onto fusible adhesive. Refer to Fusible Appliqué Preparations, pages 6–7, for instructions.

1. Lay the fusible adhesive, paper side up, over each appliqué template, and trace the shape onto the paper. Transfer any information on the template pattern to the paper, including the placement and stitching lines. Leave approximately ¼˝ of space around each piece for cutting.

2. Use paper-cutting scissors to roughly cut out all of the pieces outside the traced lines.

3. Following the manufacturer's instructions for fusing, fuse the template pieces, paper side up, onto the wrong side of the appliqué fabric pieces. Don't fuse until all of the pieces are arranged to fit on the fabric.

4. Neatly cut out all of the appliqués from the fused fabrics. Transfer the placement and stitching lines onto the right side of the fabric.

POSITIONING AND FUSING THE APPLIQUÉS

1. Remove the paper backing from the appliqués.

2. Referring to the project photo, page 17, arrange all the appliqué pieces on the quilt top. Be sure to place the fusible side of the fabric against the block. Finger-press them into place. When centering the letters on the blue background, remember that there is a ¼˝-wide seam allowance on the raw edges to the left side, top, and bottom for binding. Center the letters accordingly. Also note that the right side of the pot of gold will extend beyond the right edge of the rainbow.

3. Cut away the excess only after you are satisfied with the arrangement of all of the appliqués; fuse them into place. Always follow the fusible adhesive manufacturer's instructions.

QUILTING AND FINISHING

1. Sandwich the batting between the quilt top and backing, and quilt as desired. If necessary, refer to Layering and Quilting, page 7. I quilted over the entire surface with a loopy meandering path.

2. Once you are finished with the general quilting, begin satin stitching the details. If you're new to satin-stitched appliqué, be sure to practice stitching on scraps first, adjusting your stitch width and length until you get the look you desire. I use a very short stitch length and a width of 2.5–3.0 to make a prominent black "stroke." Follow the traced stitching detail lines and zigzag over the raw edge of all of the appliqués.

3. Refer to the project photo, page 17, and the layout, page 19, for the cross sparkle placement. Trace the shapes on the right side of the fabric, and use metallic gold thread to satin stitch cross sparkles on selected coins.

4. I look at the quilt in layers and try to stitch the uppermost "layers," such as the coins in the pot, last. In this case, though, I would stitch around the highlight of the pot first, as other stitching lines need to cross on top it.

 When you begin a line of satin stitching, pull the "tail" of your thread to the front of the presser foot so that you stitch over it as you move forward. This eliminates ugly loose threads and prevents the stitching from coming loose. Also, if you use black thread, a permanent black marker with a fine tip can help to hide any gaps in your stitching.

5. Finish the banner with the green binding strips by following the instructions in Binding, pages 7–8.

19½″ × 36″ • Quilt top made by Gary Rushton and Patrick Lose • Quilted by Patrick Lose

A contemporary salute to the Fourth of July, this quilted wall
hanging turned out to be my favorite project in the book.
I love the graphic nature of it and the way the textural red,
ivory, and blue fabrics give it the illusion of motion.

FABRIC AND SUPPLIES

Red: ½ yard for stripes and binding

Ivory: 1¼ yards for stripes, backing, letters, and stars

Navy: ½ yard for star background and letter block

Batting: 22½″ × 39″

Fusible adhesive (18″ wide): ⅔ yard

CUTTING FABRICS

From Red:

Cut 3 strips 2″ × width of fabric for the red stripes.

Cut 3 strips 2½″ × width of fabric for the binding.

From Ivory:

Cut 4 strips 2″ × width of fabric for the ivory stripes.

Cut 1 rectangle 22½″ × 39″ for the backing.

Set aside the remainder of the ivory for the letter and star appliqués.

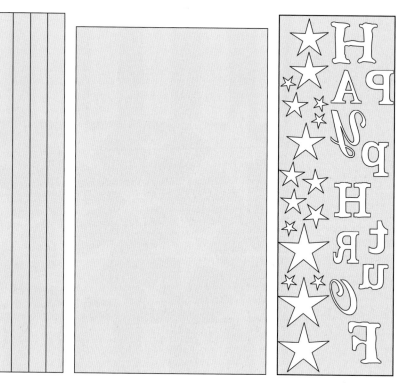

From Navy:

Cut 2 rectangles 5½″ × 20″ for the letter blocks.

Cut 1 rectangle 10½″ × 20″ for the star background block.

PIECING THE BANNER

1. Stitch the long sides of the 2″-wide ivory and red strips together to create a striped block, beginning with an ivory strip and alternating colors. Press toward the red side. Cut the block in half, as the dashed line indicates.

2. Stitch the 2 halves together to create a block with 12 stripes, beginning with the ivory strip and ending with a red strip. Press the seams toward the red side.

3. Cut the remaining ivory strip in half, and stitch it to the red end of the striped block. Press toward the red strip.

4. Cut the new striped block in half again to create 2 striped blocks. Square and trim the blocks to measure 8½″ × 20″.

5. Stitch one of the long sides of the 5½″ × 20″ navy upper letter block to one of the long sides of one of the striped blocks, right sides together, using a ¼″-wide seam. Press the seam allowance to the navy side.

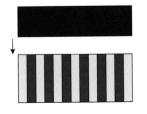

6. Repeat Step 5 to stitch the 5½″ × 20″ navy lower letter block to the bottom of the remaining striped block. Press toward the navy side.

7. In the same manner, stitch the 10½″ × 20″ navy block between the 2 striped blocks.

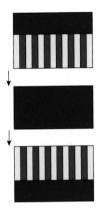

CREATING THE APPLIQUÉS

All of the appliqué template pieces are in the pullout section. They are printed actual size and are reversed for tracing onto fusible adhesive. Refer to Fusible Appliqué Preparations, pages 6–7, for instructions.

1. Lay the fusible adhesive, paper side up, over each of the star and letter appliqué templates, and trace the shapes onto the paper. Be sure to trace the placement and stitching lines also. Leave approximately ¼″ cutting space around each piece. Write the color and placement information on each piece as you trace. Trace 2 of each of the letters that indicate 2, and 1 of each of rest of the letters and the number indicated for the stars.

2. Use paper-cutting scissors to roughly cut out all of the pieces outside the traced lines.

3. Following the manufacturer's instructions for fusing, fuse the traced template pieces, paper side up, onto the wrong side of the remaining ivory fabric. Don't fuse them until all the pieces are arranged to fit on the fabrics.

4. Neatly cut out all of the appliqués from the fabric, and remove any paper backing.

POSITIONING AND FUSING THE APPLIQUÉS

1. Use the star background template pattern in the pullout section as a reference for positioning the star appliqués onto the navy center block. When you are satisfied with the positions, cut off any of the appliqués that extend beyond the banner in line with the raw edge. Fuse the star appliqués into place.

2. Referring to the project photo, page 21, arrange the letters in their respective blocks. Don't place the letters within the ¼˝-wide seam allowance you'll use for the binding. Fuse them into place.

QUILTING AND FINISHING

1. Sandwich the batting between the quilt top and backing, and quilt as desired. If necessary, refer to Layering and Quilting, page 7. I used a rayon twist thread in 2 shades of tan and meandered over the banner, being mindful to catch the points of the stars as much as possible.

2. Finish the banner with the red binding strips by following the instructions in Binding, pages 7–8.

A WARM WELCOME

14″ × 30″ • Quilt top made by Gary Rushton and Patrick Lose • Quilted by Patrick Lose

Late-summer sunflowers offer a warm welcome in this door banner that
I finished in an afternoon. It's another one of my favorites because of
the color and simplicity of the design and its cheerful appeal.

FABRIC AND SUPPLIES

Green 1: ¾ yard for flower stems, backing, and binding

Blue: ⅓ yard for sunflower background

Green 2: ⅓ yard for Welcome background

Yellow 1: 14″ × 16″ rectangle for letters and flowers 2, 3, and 5

Yellow 2: 8″ × 14″ rectangle for flowers 1 and 4

Brown 1: 7″ × 9″ rectangle for centers 2, 3, and 5

Brown 2: 5″ × 9″ rectangle for centers 1 and 4

Batting: 17″ × 33″

Fusible adhesive (18″ wide): 1 yard

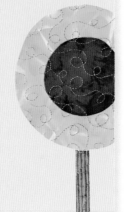

CUTTING FABRICS

From Green 1:

Cut 3 strips 2½″ × width of fabric for the binding.

Cut 1 rectangle 17″ × 33″ for the backing.

From Blue:

Cut 1 rectangle 8½″ × 30½″ for the sunflower background.

From Green 2:

Cut 1 rectangle 6½″ × 30½″ for the letter background.

CREATING THE APPLIQUÉS

All of the appliqué template pieces are in the pullout section. They are printed actual size and are reversed for tracing onto fusible adhesive. Refer to Fusible Appliqué Preparations, pages 6–7, for instructions.

1. To make the flower stem appliqués, cut a 2″ × 18″ strip from the fusible adhesive.

2. Following the manufacturer's instructions, fuse this strip to the wrong side of a remaining piece of Green 1.

3. Using a rotary cutter and ruler, cut 3 strips ½″ × 18″ from the fused fabric. Set these aside.

4. To make the remainder of the appliqués, lay the fusible adhesive, paper side up, over each appliqué template, and trace the templates onto the paper. Leave approximately ¼″ cutting space around each piece.

5. Use paper-cutting scissors to roughly cut out all of the pieces outside the traced lines.

6. Following the manufacturer's instructions for fusing, fuse the traced template pieces, paper side up, onto the wrong side of the fabrics you've chosen for your appliqués. Don't fuse them until all the pieces are arranged to fit on the fabrics.

7. Neatly cut out all of the appliqués from the fused fabrics.

8. If you don't trust your own eye, be sure to trace the placement lines for the flower centers on the right side of the fabric.

POSITIONING AND FUSING THE APPLIQUÉS

1. Remove the paper backing from the appliqués.

2. Position the centers on their corresponding flowers, and finger-press them into place.

3. Referring to the project photo, page 25, for placement, arrange the flower appliqués on the blue background first. Place the straight edges of the flowers against the raw edges of the background. Finger press them into place enough that they don't move around.

4. You should be able to make all of the flower stems from the 3 strips you cut earlier. The stems are positioned, and the excess is cut away, leaving enough for the flower to overlap the stem end by about ¼˝.

5. When you're satisfied with the positions of all of the appliqués, fuse them into place. Always follow the fusible adhesive manufacturer's instructions for fusing.

6. Position and fuse the letters on the green background in the same manner. When centering the letters on the green background, remember that there is a ¼˝-wide seam allowance on the raw edges to the left, top, and bottom for binding. Center the letters accordingly.

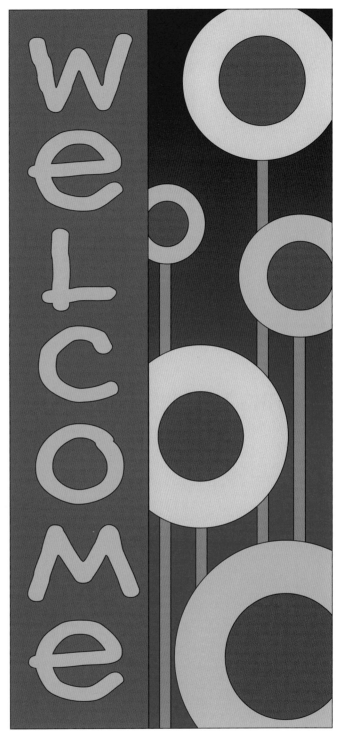

JOINING THE BACKGROUNDS

With right sides together, and using a ¼″ seam, join the 2 appliqué blocks. Press the seam allowance to one side.

QUILTING AND FINISHING

1. Sandwich the batting between the quilt top and backing, and quilt as desired. If necessary, refer to Layering and Quilting, page 7. I used a green and tan twist thread and stitched a fairly dense looped path over the entire top.

2. Finish the banner with the green binding strips by following the instructions in Binding, pages 7–8.

HAPPY BIRTHDAY

20″ × 24″ • Quilt top made by Nora Hart and Patrick Lose • Quilted by Patrick Lose

Make someone's birthday extra special with a gift that goes together in a hurry, or keep it around to hang for all of the birthday parties at your house.

FABRIC AND SUPPLIES

Turquoise: ½ yard for background and corner block

Purple: ¼ yard or fat quarter for vertical and horizontal border blocks

Lavender: ⅝ yard for binding and upper and lower cake appliqués

White: 2″ × 4″ rectangle for candle

Green: 2″ × 4″ rectangle for 4 confetti pieces

Orange: 3″ × 5″ rectangle for 4 confetti pieces and inner candle flame

Aqua 1: 4½″ × 8″ rectangle for candle glow

Aqua 2: 6½″ × 14″ rectangle for cake stand

Yellow: 9″ × 9″ square for stars and candle flame

Light lavender 1: 9″ × 11″ rectangle for frosting

Light lavender 2: 1/8 yard for letters

Backing and batting: 23″ × 27″

Fusible adhesive (18″ wide): 1 yard

CUTTING FABRICS

From Turquoise:

Cut 1 rectangle 16½″ × 20½″ for the background.

Cut 1 square 4½″ × 4½″ for the corner block.

From Purple:

Cut 1 rectangle 4½″ × 20½″ for the vertical border block.

Cut 1 rectangle 4½″ × 16½″ for the horizontal border block.

From Lavender:

Cut 3 strips 2½″ × width of fabric for the binding.

Cut 1 square 10″ × 10″ for upper and lower cake appliqués.

CREATING THE APPLIQUÉS

All of the appliqué template pieces are in the pullout section. They are printed actual size and are reversed for tracing onto fusible adhesive. Refer to Fusible Appliqué Preparations, pages 6–7, for instructions.

1. Lay the fusible adhesive, paper side up, over each appliqué template, and trace the shapes onto the paper. Be sure to trace the placement and stitching lines also. Leave approximately ¼″ cutting space around each piece. Trace 2 of each of the letters that indicate 2, and 1 each of the rest of the letters.

2. Use paper-cutting scissors to roughly cut out all of the pieces outside the traced lines.

3. Following the manufacturer's instructions for fusing, fuse the traced template pieces, paper side up, onto the wrong side of the fabrics you've chosen for your appliqués. Don't fuse them until all the pieces are arranged to fit on the fabrics.

4. Neatly cut out all of the appliqués from the fused fabrics. Transfer the placement and stitching lines onto the right side of the fabric.

5. Remove the paper backing from the cake-stand appliqué, and position the appliqué at the bottom center of the turquoise background block, using the project photo, page 29, for reference and aligning the bottom of the "stem" with the raw edge of the background.

6. Following the manufacturer's instructions for the fusible adhesive, fuse only the cake-stand appliqué into place before proceeding; the rest of the appliqués will be added later.

PIECING THE BANNER

1. Stitch one of the long sides of the vertical border block to one of the long sides of the background block, right sides together, using a ¼″-wide seam. Press the seam allowance toward the purple side.

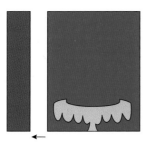

2. Stitch one of the sides of the corner block to one of the short sides of the horizontal border block, right sides together, using a ¼″-wide seam. Press the seam allowance toward the purple side.

3. Stitch the 2 pieces together to complete the top. Press.

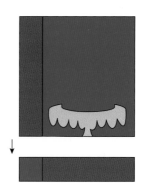

POSITIONING AND FUSING THE APPLIQUÉS

1. Remove the paper backing from the remaining appliqués.

2. Referring to the project photo, page 29, arrange all of the appliqués on the quilt top. When centering the letters and the corner block's star, remember that there is a ¼″-wide seam allowance on all sides for the binding. The straight edge of the candle's glow is aligned with the raw edge of the top.

3. When you're satisfied with the arrangement of the appliqués, fuse them into place. Always follow the fusible adhesive manufacturer's instructions.

QUILTING AND FINISHING

1. Sandwich the batting between the quilt top and backing, and quilt as desired. If necessary, refer to Layering and Quilting, page 7. I used a silver metallic thread and free-motion quilting to outline each of the pieces by going around them several times in a "scribbled" manner. I treated the detail lines the same way in the cake frosting, the cake-stand appliqués, and the drip on the side of the candle. I quilted spirals in the star centers.

2. Finish the banner with the lavender binding strips by following the instructions in Binding, pages 7–8.

HALLOWEEN HAG

18″ × 24″ • Quilt top made by Sharron Meyer and Patrick Lose • Quilted by Patrick Lose

Satin-stitch appliqué in black rayon thread gives this cartoon
Halloween hag the expression she needs to say, "Best witches
and happy haunting!" to all of the little beggars.

FABRIC AND SUPPLIES

Purple 1: 1 yard for borders, backing, and binding

Yellow 1: fat quarter for border, background, and stars

Orange: 6″ × 22″ rectangle for border squares

Black 1: 8″ × 8″ square for corner blocks

Black 2: 14″ × 14″ square for hat crown and upper brim and pupils

Green: 10″ × 15″ rectangle for hag's face

Rusty brown: 9″ × 15″ rectangle for hair

White: 8″ × 8″ square for moon, eyes, and tooth

Gray: 8″ × 7″ rectangle for underside of hat brim

Purple 2: 4″ × 7″ rectangle for hat band

Batting: 21″ × 27″

Fusible adhesive (18″ wide): 1 yard

Tear-away stabilizer: 19″ × 25″

CUTTING FABRICS

From Purple:

Cut 3 strips 2½″ × width of fabric for the binding and 2 strips 1½″ × width of fabric for the left and right borders.

From the remaining purple, cut a block 22″ wide × width of fabric as indicated by the dashed line. From this block, cut 1 rectangle 22″ × 28″ for the backing and 4 strips 1½″ × 22″ for the top and bottom borders.

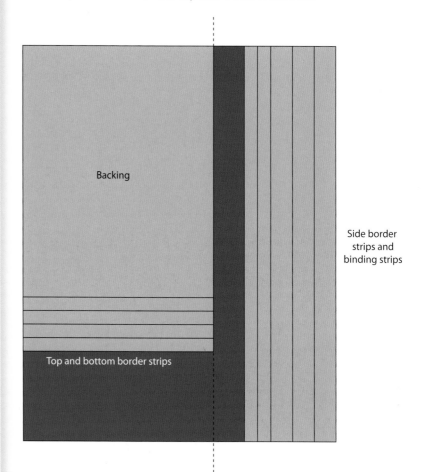

Backing

Side border strips and binding strips

Top and bottom border strips

From Yellow:

Cut 3 strips 1½″ × 22″ for the border squares and the 12½″ × 18½″ background for the witch. Set aside the remainder for the corner block stars.

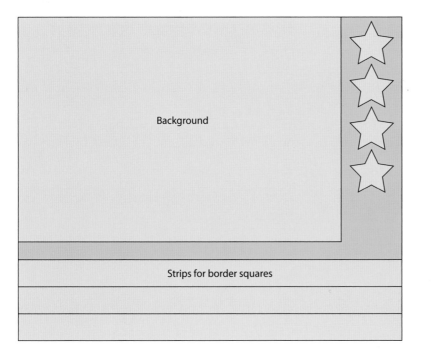

From Orange:

Cut 3 strips 1½″ × 22″ for the border squares.

From Black 1:

Cut 4 squares 3½″ × 3½″ for the border squares.

CREATING THE BORDERS

In all of the steps below, all stitching is done with the right sides of the fabrics together and using a ¼″-wide seam allowance.

1. Cut a 12½″ length from each of the 3 orange and 3 yellow strips cut for the squares. Save the remaining lengths for Step 6.

2. Stitch the strips together, beginning with a yellow strip and alternating colors to form a 6½″ × 12½″ striped block. Press the seam

allowances toward the orange strips. Trim the ends to make the block exactly 6½″ × 12″ finished.

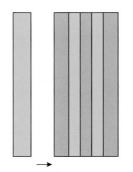

3. Cut across the striped block, as indicated by the dashed line, to form 2 blocks that are 6½″ × 6″.

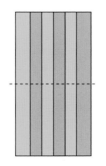

4. Join these blocks. Be sure to join the orange end to the yellow end so that the colors alternate across the block. Press the seam allowance toward the orange strip. The new block should be 12½″ × 6″.

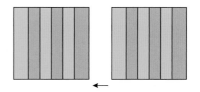

5. Cut this block into 4 strips 1½″ × 12½″ wide. Set aside 2 of these strips to be used for the top and bottom borders. Length needs to be added to the other 2.

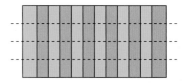

6. Cut 6 orange and 6 yellow 1½″ × 1½″ squares from the remainder of the strips that were cut in Step 1 of this section.

7. Add the squares to the ends of the 2 strips from Step 5, alternating colors. Make 2 strips, each with 18 squares, to be used for the side borders. One end of the border has a yellow square, and the other should have an orange one. Press.

8. To each side of the strips of alternating squares, stitch 1 of the 1½″-wide purple strips. Press. Trim the purple strips. Repeat for the other long strip and 2 short strips of alternating squares.

9. Stitch the corner blocks to each end of the top and bottom borders. Press the seams toward the black corners.

PIECING THE BACKGROUND

1. Stitch the side borders to the background. Press.

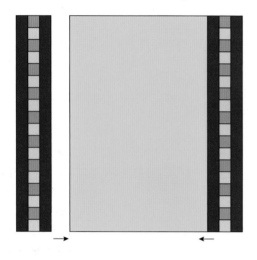

2. Complete the background by adding the top and bottom borders. Press.

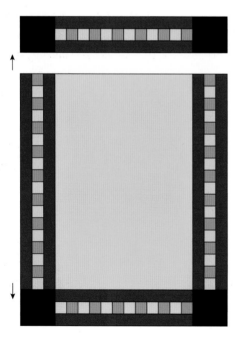

CREATING THE APPLIQUÉS

All of the appliqué template pieces are in the pullout section. They are printed actual size and are reversed for tracing onto fusible adhesive. Refer to Fusible Appliqué Preparations, pages 6–7, for instructions.

1. Lay the fusible adhesive, paper side up, over each appliqué template, and trace the shape onto the paper. If you don't trust your own eye, be sure to trace the placement and stitching detail lines also. Leave approximately ¼″ cutting space around each piece. Be sure to trace multiples if the template indicates to cut more than 1.

2. Use paper-cutting scissors to roughly cut out all of the pieces outside the traced lines.

3. Following the manufacturer's instructions for fusing, fuse the traced template pieces, paper side up, onto the wrong side of the fabrics you've chosen for your appliqués. Don't fuse them until all the pieces are arranged to fit on the fabrics.

4. Neatly cut out all of the appliqués from the fused fabrics. Transfer the placement and stitching lines onto the right side of the fabric.

POSITIONING AND FUSING THE APPLIQUÉS

1. Remove the paper backing from the appliqués.

2. Referring to the project photo, page 33, arrange all of the appliqués on the quilt top. Finger press them into place as you go, but do not fuse them until you are happy with the arrangement. When centering the stars in the corner blocks, remember that there is a ¼″-wide seam allowance on the raw edges of the black squares for the binding. The straight edges of several of the pieces should be aligned with the raw edges of the background. They will be encased in the binding.

3. When you're satisfied with the arrangement of the appliqués, fuse them into place. Always follow the fusible adhesive manufacturer's instructions.

thread, a permanent black marker with a fine tip can help to hide a lot of sins in your stitching!

tip When you begin a line of satin stitching, pull the "tail" of your thread to the front of the presser foot so that you stitch over it as you move forward. This eliminates ugly loose threads and prevents the stitching from coming loose.

1. Center the fused quilt top on the sheet of tear-away stabilizer. You can pin it in place with safety pins to keep the layers from shifting.

2. Following the traced stitching detail lines and zigzagging over the raw edges of the appliqués, begin satin stitching the details. I started with the witch's pupils and then the whites of her eyes and moved outward from there. If the stabilizer becomes clumsy, you can carefully tear it away from within the areas you are finished stitching.

3. I look at the quilt in layers and try to stitch the uppermost layers last. For example, I would stitch the hair before stitching the hat brim, which is an upper layer. That way, the ends of the stitching lines in the hair are covered by a continuous line of stitching on the brim.

4. Be sure to remove all of the tear-away stabilizer when you finish the satin stitching. Press to smooth the top.

QUILTING AND FINISHING

1. Sandwich the batting between the quilt top and backing, and quilt as desired. If necessary, refer to Layering and Quilting, page 7. I quilted around the basic shapes of the design and also stitched in a zigzag line through the squares in the border.

2. Finish the banner with the purple binding strips by following the instructions in Binding, pages 7–8.

SATIN-STITCH APPLIQUÉ AND DETAILING

Many of the details in this piece wouldn't be conveyed without some detail stitching. I chose to use satin stitching because it gives a strong outline. You can vary your stitch width, as I did, for more interest. An example of this is the way the waves in the hair are stitched in a slightly narrower line than the outline of the entire hair appliqué.

Refer to the steps below to add satin-stitching details, or—if you prefer—to *Proud To Be Irish*, Quilting and Finishing, page 20, to add satin stitching during the quilting process.

If you're new to satin-stitch appliqué, be sure to practice stitching on scraps first, adjusting your stitch width and length until you get the look you desire. If you use black

AWESOME AUTUMN

14″ × 30″ • Quilt top made by Katie Fjell, Gary Rushton, and Patrick Lose • Quilted by Patrick Lose

"Scribble" quilting in bright copper metallic thread
pulled all of the colors together in this classically
themed autumn banner of falling oak leaves.

FABRIC AND SUPPLIES

Rusty brown: ½ yard for upper and lower block, 1 leaf, and binding

Grape: ½ yard for background

Gold: ¼ yard for letters and 1 leaf

Dark green: 9″ × 11″ rectangle for leaf

Light green: 9″ × 9″ square for leaf

Red: 8″ × 10″ rectangle for leaf

Orange: 9″ × 12″ rectangle for leaf

Backing and batting: 17″ × 33″

Fusible adhesive (18″ wide): ¾ yard

CUTTING FABRICS

From Rusty Brown:

Cut 3 strips 2½″ × width of fabric for the binding.

Cut 2 rectangles 4½″ × 14½″ for the top and bottom.

From Grape:

Cut 1 rectangle 14½″ × 22½″ for the background.

PIECING THE BANNER

1. Stitch one of the long sides of the upper block to one of the short sides of the background block, right sides together, using a ¼″-wide seam. Press the seam allowance to one side.

2. Repeat Step 1 to stitch the lower block to the bottom of the background block. Press.

CREATING THE APPLIQUÉS

All of the appliqué template pieces are in the pullout section. They are printed actual size and are reversed for tracing onto fusible adhesive. Refer to Fusible Appliqué Preparations, pages 6–7, for instructions.

1. Lay the fusible adhesive, paper side up, over each appliqué template, and trace the shape onto the paper. Be sure to trace the placement and stitching lines also. Leave approximately ¼″ cutting space around each piece. Transfer any information on each piece as you trace. Trace 2 of each of the letters that indicate 2, and 1 of each of rest of the letters and the leaves.

2. Use paper-cutting scissors to roughly cut out all of the pieces outside the traced lines.

3. Following the manufacturer's instructions for fusing, fuse the traced template pieces, paper side up, onto the wrong side of the fabrics you've chosen for your appliqués. Don't fuse them until all the pieces are arranged to fit on the fabrics.

4. Cut out all of the appliqués from the fused fabrics. Transfer the placement and stitching lines onto the right side of the fabric.

POSITIONING AND FUSING THE APPLIQUÉS

1. Remove the paper backing from the letter and leaf appliqués.

2. Referring to the project photo, page 38, arrange all of the appliqués on the quilt top. When centering the Awesome Autumn letters, remember that there is a ¼˝-wide seam allowance on all sides for the binding.

3. The straight edges of the leaves align with the banner's raw edge. Note that some of the leaves extend into the top and bottom word blocks.

4. When you're satisfied with the arrangement of the appliqués, fuse them into place. Always follow the fusible adhesive manufacturer's instructions.

QUILTING AND FINISHING

1. Sandwich the batting between the quilt top and backing, and quilt as desired. If necessary, refer to Layering and Quilting, page 7. I used a copper metallic thread and free-motion quilting to outline each of the leaves by going around them several times in a "scribbled" manner. I quilted the veins of the leaves in the same way. I used a meandering path to quilt over the letters in the word blocks.

2. Finish the banner with the rusty brown binding strips by following the instructions in Binding, pages 7–8.

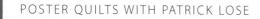

20″ × 34″ • **Quilt top made by Beverly Bruder and Patrick Lose • Quilted by Patrick Lose**

This wallhanging has a uniquely shaped top and bottom
that's easy to bind with bias-cut strips. Once your binding is
attached, it's easy to feed a shaped-to-fit wire through and coil
the ends for a whimsical hanger.

FABRIC AND SUPPLIES

Eggnog: 1¼ yards for quilt top (background) and backing

Green 1: ⅝ yard for binding strips (strips will be cut on the bias)

Green 2: ¼ yard for holly leaves

Red: ¼ yard or fat quarter for letters and berries

Batting: 23″ × 37″

Fusible adhesive (18″ wide): ⅔ yard

Wire for curly hanger: 1 yard (optional)

CUTTING FABRICS

From Eggnog:

Cut 1 rectangle 20½″ × 34½″ for the background (the long side of the banner parallel and close to the selvage). Trim the raw edges straight, and set aside the remainder for the backing.

From Green 1:

Cut 2½″-wide bias strips, and stitch the strips end to end to make 1 bias strip approximately 130″ long.

PREPARING THE BACKGROUND

Use the template provided to shape the top and bottom of the banner.

1. Fold the 20½″ × 34½″ background in half lengthwise by bringing the long raw edges together.

2. Trace the template for the top and bottom edges onto an 8½″ × 11″ sheet of paper.

3. Cut out the template along the traced line.

4. Place the template onto the background fabric so that the top of the curve is aligned with the raw edge of the top of the background, and the straight edge of the side of the template aligns with the side of the background.

5. Cut away the portion of the background that is indicated. Do **not** cut along the long straight edge of the bottom of the template.

6. Repeat Steps 4 and 5 to shape the bottom of the banner.

7. Open the background and, if desired, transfer the holly and berry placement lines onto the front of the background with a nonpermanent marking pencil or transfer paper.

CREATING THE APPLIQUÉS

All of the appliqué template pieces are in the pullout section. They are printed actual size and are reversed for tracing onto fusible adhesive. Refer to Fusible Appliqué Preparations, pages 6–7, for instructions.

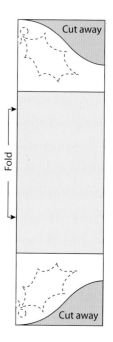

1. Lay the fusible adhesive, paper side up, over the holly, berry, and letter appliqué templates, and trace the shapes onto the paper side. Leave approximately ¼″ cutting space around each piece. If a template has a number on it, trace that many of the template onto the paper backing of the fusible adhesive. Otherwise, trace 1.

2. Use paper-cutting scissors to roughly cut out all of the pieces outside the traced lines.

3. Following the manufacturer's instructions for fusing, fuse the traced template pieces, paper side up, onto the wrong side of the fabrics you've chosen for your appliqués. Don't fuse them until all the pieces are arranged to fit on the fabrics.

4. Neatly cut out all of the appliqués from the fused fabrics. Transfer the placement and stitching lines onto the right side of the fabric.

POSITIONING AND FUSING THE APPLIQUÉS

1. Remove the paper backing from the appliqués.

2. Referring to the project photo, page 41, arrange all of the appliqués on the quilt top. When positioning the holly and berries, remember that there is a ¼″-wide seam allowance on all sides for the binding.

3. When you're satisfied with the arrangement of the appliqués, fuse them into place. Always follow the fusible adhesive manufacturer's instructions.

QUILTING AND FINISHING

1. Sandwich the batting between the quilt top and backing. Cut away the excess, leaving about 1½″ extending beyond the raw edges of the quilt top. Quilt as desired. If necessary, refer to Layering and Quilting, page 7. I used an ecru thread and free-motion quilted in a fairly tight, looped path.

2. Finish the banner with the green bias strip. Fold the binding strip in half lengthwise with wrong sides together. Press. The binding strips will be sewn to the sides, then to the top and bottom. Place the folded binding strip on the right side of the quilt top along one side edge. Stitch through all the layers, using a ¼″-wide seam allowance. Cut off the ends of the binding to match the top and bottom edges.

3. Trim the backing and batting side edge so all the layers are even with the quilt top. Turn the binding over the edge and stitch it in place. Repeat for the other side.

4. Sew the binding strip to the top of the quilt, leaving ½″ extra on both ends. Fold under the excess binding, matching the quilt edge. Trim the backing and batting even with the quilt top. Turn the binding over the edge and stitch it in place. This will leave a finished opening on the top binding side edge for the wire. Repeat for the bottom binding strip.

5. Insert the wire into the top binding side opening, cut to the desired length, and curl the ends.

SNOW DAY

14˝ × 30˝ • Quilt top made by Gary Rushton and Patrick Lose • Quilted by Patrick Lose

This quilt is great as a door banner that can be displayed throughout the winter season when the rest of the holiday décor has to be put away. It's a friendly and heartwarming greeting to chilly visitors.

FABRIC AND SUPPLIES

Grape: ¼ yard for Snow Day background

Blue: ⅓ yard for snow scene background

Light blue: ¼ yard for binding and hex snowflakes

White: 1 fat quarter for snowman and snowflakes

Lavender: ⅛ yard for letters

Black: 3″ × 8″ rectangle for snowman's eyes and mouth

Orange: 3″ × 8″ rectangle for carrot

Red: 3″ × 5″ rectangle for earmuff

Green: 3″ × 5″ rectangle for hat cuff

Light green: 2″ × 3″ rectangle for hat top

Batting: 17″ × 33″

Fusible adhesive (18″ wide): 1 yard

CUTTING FABRICS

From Grape:

Cut 1 rectangle 6½″ × 30½″ for the letter background.

From Blue:

Cut 1 rectangle 8½″ × 30½″ for the snow scene background.

From Light Blue:

Cut 3 strips 2½″ × width of fabric for the binding and hex snowflakes. (These can also be cut from scraps of various light blues.)

CREATING THE APPLIQUÉS

All of the appliqué template pieces are in the pullout section. They are printed actual size and are reversed for tracing onto fusible adhesive. Refer to Fusible Appliqué Preparations, pages 6–7, for instructions.

1. Lay the fusible adhesive, paper side up, over each appliqué template, and trace the shape onto the paper. If you don't trust your own eye, be sure to trace the placement lines on the snowman's face also. Leave approximately ¼″ cutting space around each piece.

2. Use paper-cutting scissors to roughly cut out all of the pieces outside the traced lines.

3. Following the manufacturer's instructions for fusing, fuse the traced template pieces, paper side up, onto the wrong side of the fabrics you've chosen for your appliqués. Don't fuse them until all the pieces are arranged to fit on the fabrics.

4. Neatly cut out all of the appliqués from the fused fabrics. Be sure to keep the unconnected pieces of the snowflakes with their large pieces.

5. Remove the paper backing from the snowman, upper corner snowflake, earmuff, hat cuff, and hat top.

6. The appliqués in Step 5 fall into either the seam allowance for the binding or the seam allowance used to join the 2 background pieces. Position these appliqués onto the blue background, referring to the project photo, page 44, and aligning the straight edges with the raw edges of the background.

7. When you're satisfied with the arrangement of the appliqués, fuse them into place following the manufacturer's instructions for the fusible web you're using.

PIECING THE BANNER

Stitch one of the long sides of the blue background block to one of the long sides of the grape background block, right sides together, using a ¼˝-wide seam. Press the seam allowance to one side.

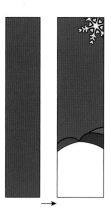

POSITIONING AND FUSING THE APPLIQUÉS

1. Remove the paper backing from the remaining appliqués.

2. Referring to the project photo, page 44, arrange all of the appliqués on the quilt top. When centering the letters, remember that there is a ¼˝-wide seam allowance on the raw edges of the grape background for the binding. Note that the snowman's carrot nose and a couple of points on the large snowflake jump the seam joining the 2 background blocks.

3. When you're satisfied with the arrangement of the appliqués, fuse them into place. Always follow the fusible adhesive manufacturer's instructions.

QUILTING AND FINISHING

1. Sandwich the batting between the quilt top and backing, and quilt as desired. If necessary, refer to Layering and Quilting, page 7. I gave the banner a little sparkle by using an opalescent metallic white top thread and free-motion quilting. I stitched a fairly dense loopy path over the snow scene and a meandering path over the words.

2. Finish the banner with the light blue binding strips by following the instructions in Binding, pages 7–8.

RESOURCES

Also by Patrick Lose:

For a list of other fine books from C&T Publishing, ask for a free catalog:

C&T PUBLISHING, INC.

P.O. Box 1456

Lafayette, CA 94549

(800) 284-1114

Email: ctinfo@ctpub.com

Website: www.ctpub.com

C&T Publishing's professional photography services are now available to the public. Visit us at www.ctmediaservices.com.

For quilting supplies:

COTTON PATCH

1025 Brown Ave.

Lafayette, CA 94549

Store: (925) 284-1177

Mail order: (925) 283-7883

Email: CottonPa@aol.com

Website: www.quiltusa.com

Note: Fabrics used in the quilts shown may not be currently available, as fabric manufacturers keep most fabrics in print for only a short time.

ABOUT THE AUTHOR

Patrick has spent his professional years in a variety of creative fields. He began his career as an actor and singer, which eventually led him to designing costumes for stage and screen. Costuming credits include more than 50 productions and work with celebrities such as Liza Minnelli and Jane Seymour.

An artist and illustrator since childhood, Patrick works in many mediums. When he sits down to "doodle" at the drawing board, he never knows what one of his designs might become. But whether it's designing quilts, wearable art, stationery products, or home décor, he enjoys creating it all.

He is probably most well-known for his very successful and long-running collections of fabric from Timeless Treasures and Moda that include his trademark marbleized solids, which are trendsetters in the industry. Patrick's quilts, crafts, clothing, and home-decorating accessories have appeared in such distinguished magazines as *Better Homes & Gardens*, *American Patchwork and Quilting*, *Country Crafts*, *Christmas Ideas*, *Halloween Tricks & Treats*, and many more. He has also written books on quilting and crafting for C&T Publishing and Sterling Publishing and has appeared on several television programs, including *The Carol Duvall Show*, *Simply Quilts*, *America Sews*, and *Martha's Sewing Room*.

Patrick invites you to visit his website at www.patricklose.net to see what's new. You can also email him at patricklose@gmail.com.